Contents

Foreword

10 POSITIVE HABITS THAT CAN IMPROVE YOUR QUALITY OF LIFE FOREVER

What makes people successful, you may wonder? it can be said that they always need focus, personal discipline and the will to always make something great. One thing they have in common are good habits and daily rituals that they cultivate to improve their quality of life. Actually, old habits are hard to change, but if you learn and adapt to new habits they can positively improve your quality of life forever. Therefore, if you do an activity that is done repeatedly, then this habit if adopted will improve mental and physical health. Your overall feeling of well-being will increase substantially. In return, you can also enjoy a happier life, less stress and fewer health complications. Not a bad result isn't it for such a small compromise? Here are the positive habits:

CREATE A MORNING RITUAL.

Waking Up to a Better Day

Do you know how most Americans wake up? They jolt awake to an alarm, flip on bright lights, reach for their electronic devices, then dive directly into their day's activities and responsibilities. They check email and texts, scan social feeds and news headlines to see what they might have missed while they slept. Seconds after their feet hit the floor, they switch on the television or radio to hear the familiar prattle of morning-show hosts or the dire pronouncements of news anchors; they turn on loud, hyper-intense music or hop on treadmills to get their blood pumping. Others jump into productive tasks, returning emails and calls, responding to requests for information, finishing up last minute assignments before they have to go to work.

For your sanity, for your health, and for the benefit of everything you hold dear, you are going to consciously reclaim the first few moments of your day—for you. Rather than abruptly throwing some big industrial on-off lever into the on position, you're going to turn your delicate dials at a pace your body and brain can handle. And for that, you will be richly rewarded, because from here on out, every single part of your day is going to go better.

The Three-Minute Morning Ritual

Waking more gently lets you take advantage of important theta-brainwave states and ramp up more gradually toward demanding tasks. Regularly adhering to a simple morning ritual also helps you build self-efficacy, develop mindfulness and equanimity, and prepare for a successful day. It lets you start the day on your own terms. So let's do this thing!

How to Start:

- First thing on rising, before you do anything else (especially looking at your phone), choose any feel-good activity and just enjoy it for at least three minutes, or for as long as you find it rewarding and doable.
- Before and during your Morning Minutes practice, avoid all exposure to electronics, media, and other sensory distractions or stressors. No email, texts, social media, or news until your body and mind have had a chance to come gradually and peacefully into their relaxed waking state.

- Some good Morning Minutes practice options include meditation, yoga, stretching, reading poetry or wisdom literature, journaling, stepping outside to see the sunrise, listening to birds through an open window, or playing a musical instrument.
- Consider using the last few moments of your practice to set your intentions for the day and visualize how you want it to go or to reflect on the things you are most grateful for.
- Close your practice with three deep, energizing breaths. Then move on to the active part of your day, noticing how the three minutes you just invested in your own well-being changes your outlook and energy.

Why:

- This lets you preserve and take advantage of the valuable "twilight" theta-brainwave state that exists between waking and sleeping—a highly suggestible state associated with insight, creativity, healing, lucidity, and deep awareness.

- It reduces the alarm response of the sympathetic nervous system and associated inflammatory cortisol spike.
- It spares you from exposing your mind to stressful, distracting inputs and outside agendas when it is at its most impressionable.
- It builds your capacity for self-regulation and your sense of self efficacy (the belief that you can do what you set out to do).
- It empowers you to start your day on your own terms (rather than in reaction to outside forces).
- It builds your "savoring" muscles—helping you develop the neurocircuitry for experiencing and registering positive, pleasurable experiences and harvesting the downstream dopamine rewards (see research by Eric Garland, PhD, on how savoring works to counter unhealthy addictive tendencies).
- It establishes an early state of mindfulness and equanimity, making it easier to retain and reclaim that state later in the day.
- It gives you an early window of opportunity to establish your autonomy and to carry that sense of sovereignty with you as you go out to face the day.
- Notice barriers and attitudes that may be undoing other healthy intentions.
- Waking up early is not the only thing that can change a person's life for the better. But it's learning about setting a routine in the morning and doing the same on a regular basis. Having a to- do list first thing in the morning will keep you motivated and energized throughout the day. This will eliminate the delays that sometimes leave you feeling overwhelmed and not knowing what to do in the next step. In addition, a little morning exercise, meditation, yoga, reading a book and making a healthy breakfast can make you excited too. Establishing a meaningful morning ritual will help you start the day on a proactive note that has a very positive impact. After all, we are creatures of habit, why not do it regularly if it gives us pleasure?

Tips for Waking Up:

- Wake to a pleasant, non-jarring signal or sound, ideally from something that is not your smartphone. I prefer Now & Zen's progressive chime-based alarm clocks and light-based, sunrise- mimicking alarm clocks (like Philips Wake-Up Light, Lumie Bodyclock Active Wakeup Light, and MOSHE Sunrise Alarm Clock), most of which also have audible-alarm backups), but low-key, wake-to- music options can work, too—just be sure you can easily turn off, turn over, cover up, or otherwise block any light-emitting displays.
- Keeping houselights low, if possible, go directly to your practice area. If you're a person who loves coffee, hot tea, or water first thing, feel free to make your preferred morning beverage to enjoy during your practice.
- Avoid all interaction with complex electronics, digital devices, media (including radio, television, and newspapers)—and ideally, any complex interactions with other people—until your Morning Minutes practice is complete.
- Set a timer for a minimum of three minutes, take a breath, and settle yourself.
- Choose any feel-good activity (see list of suggestions below) and enjoy it for the period of time you have chosen, or for as long as desirable or doable.
- On closing, do a brief ideal-day "snapshot" visualization or set intention for the day—or just take three deep breaths—and blow out the candle.
- Notice how you did (or did not do) the practice.
- Track immediate and longer-term effects. Optional Morning Minutes Activities:

What you do during your Morning Minutes window is entirely up to you. What's important is that

you do it for a minimum of three blissful minutes.

- Meditate, pray, or do breathing exercises.
- Do yoga, stretch, foam-roller, or massage your hands and feet.
- Step outside, look at the sky, and listen to the birds or the sound of the wind.
- Pet your dog or cat.
- Play a musical instrument.
- Doodle in a sketchbook.
- Write a little poem or pen a love note to yourself or someone else.
- Envision one thing you'd like to see happen today.
- Think about three things you're grateful for, taking one deep breath for each.
- Just sit there, do nothing, and notice how that feels.

Remember, your minimum commitment for this practice is three minutes. You can go longer if you like (hey, if you can carve out the time, take a half hour or more!), but let three minutes be your base plan. Even at three minutes, you might be tempted to skip this apparently self-indulgent and unproductive practice. After all, you've got things to do! You are busy and important! People are relying on you!

The path starts right here with this small, seemingly innocuous yet revolutionary act. This is your moment.

All the more reason why this three minutes matters so mightily. How much will everyone in your world benefit from a saner and stronger you? Plenty. Keep in mind that this is how you reclaim your power to choose. This is how you train your system to do something beyond the habitual and out of the ordinary.

You're going to be doing a lot of that down the road. But the path starts right here with this small, seemingly innocuous yet revolutionary act. This is your moment.

So enjoy. For three whole minutes.

Reflection

Did you do your Three-Minute Morning Ritual? Yes? Great! How did it feel? Did you not do it?

Hmmm, interesting ... notice why. Write down the reason.

Remember—the goal is not for you to comply with any one set of steps or parameters that I

prescribe; it's for you to establish healthy patterns you can enjoy for a lifetime. This simple, quiet,

three-minute space is where all of your new patterns take root.

CHAPTER TWO

FOLLOW THE 80/20 RULE.

The 80/20 Rule Explained and How To Use It (Plus Examples)

The 80/20 rule is a prediction model applied in a variety of business settings to determine factors that affect success and improvement. It can help you optimize your workplace productivity by guiding your analysis of tasks, time allocation and responsibility delegation.

In this article, we explain what the 80/20 rule is, the benefits of using it, steps to use the 80/20 rule and how the 80/20 mindset can help you identify strategies and opportunities that benefit your career.

What is the 80/20 rule?

The 80/20 rule is a statistical principle that states 80% of results often come from approximately 20% of causes. In 1895, Italian economist Vilfredo Pareto published his findings on wealth distribution after he discovered that 20% of Italy's citizens owned 80% of the country's wealth. Since Pareto's findings, other scholars have applied his 80/20 rule of cause and effect—also known as the "Pareto principle"—to a variety of situations outside of wealth distribution, including business principles and professional development. For example, in business, it is often said that 80% of sales result from 20% of clients. While 80/20 is the most commonly found ratio, the Pareto principle may also exist in other similar ratios, such as 70/30, 75/25 or 85/15. These values all show that a low percentage of causes affect or create a high percentage of results. The benefits of using the 80/20 rule The 80/20 rule can help you identify where the majority of your time, money or energy is best spent. Using the 80/20 rule, you can determine achievable goals and outline specific tasks to reach them 7 and stay focused on what makes the most impact. Here are just a few benefits the 80/20 rule provides:

When to use the 80/20 rule

There are many ways to put the 80/20 rule into practice in your workplace. The following examples demonstrate how to use the 80/20 rule to analyze success and improvement factors and maximize efforts to achieve results.

Business management

Applying the 80/20 rule to business matters has several advantages, especially in how you can streamline the company's business model to invest in the people, products and systems that offer the biggest returns. For example: Ben is the owner of a small business that has gained popularity over the past year. To optimize his restaurant hours, Ben uses the 80/20 rule to discover that nearly 15% of the restaurant's hours yield 85% of revenue. This 15% indicates that his peak hours are between 7 p.m. and 9 p.m. Ben decides to extend his dinner service by one hour to potentially increase revenue during peak hours.

Career development

You can apply the 80/20 rule to streamline your job search, seek out the most impactful opportunities and build a strong professional network. For example: Tanya is a marketing professional re-entering the workforce after being a stay-at-home mom for four years. She wants to find a position that combines her skills in market analysis and personal interest in organic baby products. Tanya applies the 80/20 rule to her job search to use 80% of her time searching for and applying to market research jobs for infant wellness companies and 20% of her time applying to other marketing positions in other industries. With this method, Tanya streamlines her job search tasks that relate directly to her intended career path while still keeping her options open to other jobs that might lead to opportunities.

Productivity

You can use the 80/20 rule to determine which tasks yield the most significant impact and optimize your productivity for the most results. Use the Pareto principle to schedule your time, complete important tasks, set realistic deadlines and improve your focus. For example: Jolene works from home as a medical coder. Although she has the ability to set her own hours, she finds herself working late to reach deadlines. Jolene uses the 80/20 rule to identify which 25% of her daily tasks make up 75% of her week's work. She dedicates 75% of each day to the most impactful tasks, improving her time management and ability to reach critical deadlines. This principle suggests that in any situation, 20% of tasks produce 80% of results. Which means that out of all your to-do lists, the ones that create the greatest positive impact are the ones that deserve the most of your time and energy. If you focus on this 20%, you will maximize your productivity and have the freedom to focus on other activities from a similar to-do list. This will be effective in helping people who are easily distracted or rather overwhelmed by a large workload.

LEARN TO SINGLE-TASK.

What Is Single-Tasking?

Single-tasking, the opposite of multitasking, means focusing on one task at a time and getting it done before moving on to the next. It's better for productivity but harder to achieve and sustain for extended periods of time. When you single-task, you focus on one task or activity with as few distractions and interruptions as possible. The goal is to complete the task in progress or reach a specific milestone before moving on to another activity. Single-tasking improves your attention span and mental muscles. It gets you into a flow state, where you're immersed in your work. You're therefore able to perform better, produce your best work, and complete the task quicker. Single-tasking limits excessive brain stimulation. It restricts outside distractions and channels your focus to the one thing you should be working on. This creates better mental health conditions by reducing undue excitement and stress levels. Single-tasking also requires you to be present, which is more challenging when multitasking. Studies show that the human mind wanders when you don't intentionally focus it on one thing. Living in a distracted state decreases your feelings of happiness, your engagement, your productivity, and your overall well-being. Some of these benefits include: • You retain more information. • You make fewer mistakes. • You're more productive and efficient. • You feel less stress, even when working harder. • You get into a flow state. • You may experience increased positive feelings and better well-being. The Downsides of the Default Habit: Multitasking Multitasking (the opposite of single-tasking) is doing two things at once or switching rapidly between multiple tasks. Although it's thought to improve productivity, multitasking actually decreases your performance. Multitasking, particularly on complex tasks, can cause you to make avoidable mistakes. While it may seem like you're getting things done, you may be taking longer because of constant context switching and increasing cognitive load. Multitasking also increases blood pressure, stress levels, and mental health issues like anxiety and depression. These things happen as a consequence of constantly splitting your attention. When you multitask, you drain your mental energy quickly, so you have less as the workday continues

5 Steps to Develop a Single-Tasking Habit

To be successful at single-tasking, you need to keep your mind present and organized. Follow our five-step guidelines to get better at focusing on one thing at a time.

1. Make a Prioritized To-Do List

For effective single-tasking, begin each week with planning and prioritizing your tasks for each day. Starting your day without a plan opens you to distractions, procrastination, and busy work. Avoid this by making a prioritized to-do list. Consider what tasks, if completed, will have the highest impact on your goals and progress. Pick only one to three big tasks or priorities for each day so that you're more likely to complete them. Then, focus on something new the next day. Planning your workdays and weeks may require some extra time, but it pays enormous dividends in focus and productivity as you single-task through your day with a clear and organized mind.

2. Set Implementation Intentions

Setting implementation intentions means creating a specific plan that states when, where, and how you will execute a particular task. For example: • I will take deep breaths and practice mindful meditation every weekday at 12:05 p.m. during my break and 5:05 p.m. right after work. This makes it more likely that you will do it because you don't have to think about when, where, or how to do it. Set implementation intentions for your priorities and important tasks. Developing a specific plan for when, where, and how you tackle your big daily goals increases your chances of being successful.

3. Batch Your Tasks

After writing a to-do list and setting implementation intentions for the big tasks, break up the remaining time into big chunks that you can use to tackle all that's left over for the day. Batch similar, smaller tasks into dedicated time slots to reduce context switching and maintain productivity as you go through your list. This helps to retain focus on one main thing at every time during the day. You will be surprised to see how focused you can be when tasks are broken properly into sizable chunks. Follow a regular schedule to get more gains from your time blocks. You can schedule "do not disturb" hours to limit outside distractions, like your coworkers dropping in or your cell phone ringing. Schedule to-do's on your calendar so that each task gets a specific time slot. This way, you'll always know what to focus on during the day.

4. Work in Short Bursts

Working on the same thing for long periods of time can be boring and monotonous. To single-task successfully, take regular breaks between work to rest and recharge. Use the Pomodoro Technique for long, drawn-out tasks at work. With this technique, you focus on a single task for 25 minutes, then take a five-minute break. Repeat four cycles before moving on to a 10 different task. You may choose to adjust the timing based on your available time and workload. The idea is to focus on a task for as long as possible, then rest or switch to a completely new task.

5. Control Your Environment

To be successful at single-tasking, you must eliminate as much distraction as possible. Some possible ways to do this include: • Decluttering your workspace • Silencing your phone or turning it off • Turning off notifications from social media and other distracting apps • Closing tabs and apps like email and Slack on your desktop • Disabling web push notifications You can schedule dedicated blocks of time to catch up on notifications and check email. Don't shy away from practicing asynchronous communication, and don't expect instant responsiveness from yourself or others. Track Your Time to Improve Your Single-Tasking Routine If you're having a hard time completing work tasks and getting things done, single-tasking may be the strategy for you. Single-tasking improves focus and productivity, reduces the chances of mistakes, and improves mental health and well-being. The first step to successful single-tasking is to schedule designated activities at specific time slots. This helps to empty and organize your mind so you can focus on the one thing at hand. Tracking your work time provides a sturdy foundation for scheduling and executing each task. Knowing how you spend your time forces you to use it wisely and helps you better predict how much you need to complete future tasks. Are you struggling with multitasking and having trouble adopting single-tasking? Do you want to improve your focus and productivity with less stress and hassle? Download the Rize time-tracking app today. It automatically logs your work hours and productivity, and it reminds you when you need a break. Through Rize's weekly reports, you'll learn how to improve your focus, create better habits, and plan your workdays in optimal and productive ways

CHAPTER FOUR

APPRECIATE MORE.

When words of appreciation are said to people, there is a satisfaction that comes with it, an urge to do more and be the best in what they have been appreciated about. This is the same feeling that comes when you appreciate yourself. You feel loved and there is no form of disrespect that can be directed at you that you will ever take. Below are some ways to appreciate yourself more:

Meditation

Meditation is a beautiful way to centre yourself. When life is stressful or your mind is racing, you can always turn to meditation. It's also accessible to everyone because you can do it anywhere. All you need to do is find a quiet, comfortable space, close your eyes, and simply breathe. When you dedicate yourself to easing your mind every day, you will reap the benefits of meditation as your own wellness advocate

Read

Finding a book or books! that speak to you is an extremely important part of self-love and wellness for the mind. The more you read, the more you find new ways to love yourself more and more. You learn new ways, you also discover things you probably have never paid attention to about yourself.

Avoid Negativity

Where do you spend most of your time? Is it your desk at work? Is it your car? When you look around your surroundings, do you feel a burst of joy? If not, the next step is to create an environment you absolutely love. Surround yourself with positive messages, pictures of people you love, and anything that makes you feel better. It is an act of self-love when you are in a comfortable environment full of the things that bring you joy. When you can smile by just looking around, you're practicing self-love!

Gratitude

Having a morning and night-time routine that is dedicated to gratitude is an amazing way to boost your self-love. And all you need is a journal to start. When you wake up every morning and each night before you sleep, write down three things for which you're grateful. It's a beautiful way to honor yourself and your life. It's a perfect time to say thank you to your body!

CHAPTER FIVE

Do a social media detox.

How often do you reach for the phone first thing in the morning and check your Twitter notifications? How often when you're on vacation are you more concerned about taking the perfect Instagram picture than enjoying yourself? How often are you locked in an internet argument on Facebook? A social media detox gives us a bit of clarity into this. 4. The amount of mental energy we give our phones, specifically social media, could be put to much better use. 5. Social media, in its inception, was harmless fun. Now, it has evolved to be part of our daily lives. It's how we consume most of our information, and it influences everything from elections to public discourse. 6. But social media is not real life. As much influence, or seeming influence, it has, it's a curated and selective sample of what's actually going on in the world. 7. Many people are beginning to discover this. There has been a recent trend of people consciously reducing their social media use. Some have even gone full cold turkey and deleted their social media accounts. 8. However, you don't need to go cold turkey to experience the benefits of avoiding social media. A social media detox may just be enough for you if you're experiencing the anxiety and stress that comes with social media use

What is a social media detox?

A social media detox is a conscious elimination of social media use and consumption for a set period of time. Generally, most social media detoxes are 30 days, but some people do 7 days or even a year-long social media detox. Ideally, you're completely eliminating social media use and consumption. This means deleting and removing all social media apps from your phone, and in some cases where it's possible, temporarily disabling your social media accounts.

Social media detox vs. social media

break

A social media detox is different than a social media break. A break from social media accounts is a promise to yourself to stay off of sites like Facebook, Twitter, TikTok, and Instagram for a set period of time. A social media detox is a complete disconnect from social media platforms and may even include a drastic measure such as giving away the passwords to your accounts to a trusted friend or completely deleting your accounts.

Why take a social media detox

If you're here or you've been thinking about taking some time off of social media, you should probably do it, and that should be reason enough. You're reading this because you're noticing your social media usage is through the roof social media networks are affecting your self esteem and overall well being. If you feel like social media has taken over your life, if it preoccupies your mind, or if you find yourself constantly and habitually reaching for your phone, these might be signs that it's time for a break. ear your mind A social media detox gives you a chance to clear your mind. We're sucked into this online world of pretty filters on models and influencers, a friend's curated version of their life in photos and captions, and news headlines designed to spark an emotional reaction. This is all a recipe for a disaster when it comes to our mental health. It's unnecessary clutter, it's informational junk food, and ultimately most of it is useless to you besides disturbing your tranquility. Imagine how much better use of your time and mental energy could go into the things you actually care about, or changes you can actually affect on the world. Taking a break from social media gives you a chance to take a step back and really evaluate what's most important in your life and what is a much better use of your time and mental space

Take back control of your digital habits

It also gives you back control of your phone and your digital habits. Social media apps and websites are designed to get you addicted to the feedback loops, notifications, likes, and instant gratification it gives you. 13 Every time you pull down the screen and refresh, hoping for a new notification or Like, you're pulling down that slot machine arm hoping there's something new to stimulate you. And when there's a new Like, Favorite, or Comment, you get a little bit of a dopamine hit. This is intentional. These apps and websites have been optimized and iterated on for years by behavior scientists and psychologists hired by these tech companies to keep you engaged with their application. Why? So you keep coming back and stay on their platform longer. The longer you stay on their platform, and the more you keep coming back, the more ads they can serve you. The more ads they can serve you, the more money they can make from you. This creates an incentive for these tech companies to optimize their platforms against the spirit of their original intention or mission. It isn't really about connecting you with people, it's about keeping you and your brain addicted. It gets to the point where you're no longer really in control of your digital habits. It becomes compulsive. You check your feed first thing in the morning, you check it every time you geta notification, and you're glued to your screen even when you're trying to spend quality time with real people. Finally, the last reason to take a social media detox is simply the benefits of taking a break from social media. Benefits of a social media detox So, are there any real benefits to taking a social media detox? What can one expect?

More free time

When you start a social media detox, you may find yourself a little bored. That compulsion to open Twitter or Instagram whenever your phone is in your hand will need to be replaced with something. The amount of time you spend on your phone will have to be used for something else. Hopefully, something much more productive. If social media was your way to stay informed on issues you care about, instead of consuming information, why not spend this time taking action and doing something? If social media was your way to stay in touch with friends, write them a letter or spend more time in person with people you care about.

Less anxiety

Inevitably, what will happen after a week or so is with more and more mental clutter out of the way, you'll no longer fall prey to the worry of the day that makes the headlines, feeds or Trends on social media. Plenty of studies link social media and depression. With enough time, you'll find yourself being more positive since social media tends to jade us and make us more cynical. 14 You'll also find yourself comparing yourself less to other people. You'll no longer feel like you'll have to keep up with the Jones, so to speak. This will help lower your anxiety significantly. There's a lot of evidence that suggests most of today's anxiety comes from social media use and consumption. Better mornings Most people check their phones first thing in the morning, and some of those people immediately open up a social media app upon waking. They see that alert and notification and they need to investigate it. This sets the tone for the rest of the morning, and sometimes even the rest of the day. Intentionally staying away from social media forces you to use your time either in the mornings, or during your commute to work, or while your morning coffee, in a different way. Rather then spending time reading a feed, read a book. Instead of taking some photos for Instagram, take a quick morning walk. Rather than seeing what so-and-so Tweeted, notice what thoughts enter your mind with a morning meditation. More mindfulness One thing I've found when I've had to force myself off of social media for a while, was just how mindful I became of my device usage. It actually started to bother me. I caught myself several times, reaching for my phone, scrolling over to an app that I deleted. Then I found myself compulsively typing Twitter.com into my address bar before stopping myself. I became much more mindful during this period and I was no longer a zombie scrolling through feeds and moving from one social media app to another without putting much thought into it. Finally, I began to realize just how much mental real estate and time this stuff actually took from me and my life. It was pretty eye-opening. Then I began to think about how many of my friends and family are caught up in this as well. It helped me practice mindfulness more in my daily activities and routine. It forced me to be present and actually sit with the boredom and cravings I had. How to take a social media detox Here's the step-by-step process to take your first social media detox. On the surface, it may seem simple, but we're going to walk through it anyway to ensure you're set up for success with it. This guide will also help you get through your first week so that time spent is spent productively and go on without social media cold turkey. Tell people The first step to taking a social media detox is to tell people. Tell people you interact the most that you'll be offline for a while. This will do a few things. First, it will keep you accountable. If you're back within a few days Tweeting or posting photos, the people you told will hopefully call you out on it. This will help you stick with the detox. 15 Secondly, it will let people know you haven't disappeared if you wind up sticking with it. Most people won't really care, and some may not even notice you're more inactive on the social media sites they're on (don't take it personally!) Delete the apps and block the websites The next step is to delete the social media apps from your mobile devices, especially your phone. This step is required. I can almost guarantee you that you will not succeed if you keep the apps on your phone during the detox, or you try to rationalize to yourself that you'll only check them once a week. For this to work, you'll need to disconnect completely. If that seems too hard (or even impossible), try a shorter detox. You may also want to install an app or tool on your computer that can block out social media websites for you. A few suggestions we like are Freedom and Cold Turkey. You may even want to block social media apps on your mobile devices. This isn't required, but it's beneficial, especially if you check social media on your computer or laptop. If you're struggling despite deleting apps, have a trusted family member or friend change the passwords to your accounts, and only give them to you after your detox is over. This is the extreme case, but I thought it's worth putting it out there for those that need it. Plan what you will do during your detox The last step is to plan what you will do during your detox and actually fill your spare time with the things you plan to do. You may wind up surprised at how much time you'll find during the day that you otherwise would have occupied with your social media habit. If possible, try to replace your social media habit with something that doesn't involve technology. I suggest this because using your phone or laptop to replace a digital habit isn't really productive. Some suggestions that I found useful: Reading Spending time with friends and family Learning something new (language, hobby, skill) Working on a side project or business Exercising, gym, yoga Travel during your detox Also, some of the best times to meditate and practice mindfulness are when you're bored or have downtime. Go on a meditation retreat as part of your detox if you're feeling bold. 16 But if you need to replace your digital habit with a more productive digital habit, here are a few suggestions: Download Kindle on your phone and read books during downtime/boredom instead of looking at social media Listen to podcasts or audiobooks Write Take an online course How to deal with FOMO One of the most prominent objections to taking a social media detox is "how will I know what's going on?". Often, there's this sense of FOMO or "Fear of Missing Out." For some, social media is how they consume most of their news and stay informed. For others, it's how they keep in touch with friends they aren't able to see everyday in real life. If you feel like you will be out of the loop when it comes to current events and the news, don't. If something is important enough, you'll hear about it from a friend, family member, or colleague. Also, most information you consume is not actually informing you. It's distracting you. All the noise is a lot less useful than you might think. Even if you follow inspirational people on social media, turn to books, documentaries, and podcasts for a while to learn from interesting people. Finally, when it comes to staying in touch with people, we could all put a little more effort into it. During my social media detox, I pen-palled over email with long-distance friends. I also picked up the phone and called people every weekend, even just to see how they were doing for 10 minutes. Yes, it confused people at first, but eventually, after I did it every week, it deepened my connection to them. Finally, I simply tried to spend more time in person with people. Yes, everyone is busy nowadays, but I still made an effort. It was great for my mental health and my connections with people. "What if I use social media for my business or professional life?" Another common concern before starting any kind of social media detox is that people use social media platforms for their professional lives. A good tip here is to keep your work and professional life separate if possible. Create a social media account just for your business or professional persona. Detox from your personal one and ensure you're only using your business account for business. Stay connected with important clients and partners but avoid the Twitter and Facebook drama. Your turn The first step to a successful social media detox is merely trying it. Even if you're hesitant or unsure if you can do it, try it for a weekend. See how you feel after 2 or 3 consecutive days of being off of social media. Like how you feel? Try a week and slowly progress to a full month. 17 Many people find that after their social media detoxes, they never want to come back. It's often the first step to not only a much calmer and simpler life, but to disconnecting from social media for good.

CHAPTER SIX

EXERCISE OFTEN.

A person should set aside at least 15–30 minutes in a day to exercise. Countless benefits come simply by exercising. In addition to physical improvement, regular exercise can pump creativity and improve your cognitive skills. Exercise also helps reduce the risk of developing some serious health problems, such as diabetes, obesity, cholesterol etc. Exercising doesn't always have to involve lifting heavy equipment at the gym, it can also be fun activities, such as playing with pets, relaxing with friends or family, taking walks around the park, etc. Usually in the first month to create the habit of exercising it is indeed very hard and seems demanding, but if done consistently and fully committed to yourself, it will have a good impact in the long term for you, such as your social behavior will improve, your appetite is always normal, digestion become smoother, sleep more soundly, improve memory, etc.

CHAPTER SEVEN

INVEST IN SELF-CARE.

Why You Should Invest in Self Care

We all tend to lead rather busy lives. That might be running your own business or having a busy social life, whatever it might be, there is no denying that self-care can have a significant impact on your health and wellbeing. Fortunately, there is now a huge range of luxurious and indulgent natural self-care products available to take advantage of. This can include the likes of bath salts and candles that deliver amazing scents and aromas that send you into a state of relaxation, enabling you to escape the modern world and indulge in some time to yourself. With this in mind, have you ever considered the importance of self-care and what it can offer because when you invest in the right products you are also investing in yourself.

Enhance Your Physical Health

Living a busy life can take its toll on your physical health. With the right self-care routine and products, you can take care of your body. Whether it's a soak in the bath with a lit candle or the use of bath salts, you can simply unwind and relax, allowing your muscles to release those aches and pains, leaving you feeling refreshed and rejuvenated.

Melt Away Stress and Anxiety

Stress and anxiety can quickly consume us but there is a way of reducing the symptoms of both. By following a self-care routine, you can shut the world away for a while and allow yourself to be consumed by our sustainable products that can help to promote better mental health. Using different essential oils, you can alleviate anxiety and even reduce stress, all of which will help you to feel at ease.

Boost Mood and Improve Mental Health

Investing in luxurious products that deliver an unforgettable experience, you can boost your mood with different aromas and scents. Allowing yourself to drift away with aromas that lift your mood, you'll feel like a completely different person. This can help to enhance positivity and leave you feeling happier and more attuned with your body. One simple change to your self-care routine can really make a difference.

Relax and Improve Your Sleep

Sleep is especially important to both our mental and physical state. Tiredness can cause mental problems and leave us struggling to take care of daily tasks. However, self-care can teach you the importance of relaxation and how that can help to improve your sleep. If you spend time on yourself and give yourself the opportunity to unwind with the right products and routine, you'll find that you'll be able to switch off and indulge in a deeper and more rewarding sleep. The Importance of the Right Products Self-care is hugely important but to enhance the experience, the right products can have a significant impact. It is well-known that scents, aromas and essential oils can all impact how we feel and that is why it is important to include in yourself care routine, natural products which possess therapeutic properties and not ones are made with harmful chemicals. not. Once you connect with a brand and their products, you'll soon realise and feel the benefits ofself-care

CHAPTER EIGHT

READ BOOKS.

There are great benefits to always stimulating our brains on a daily basis, although some are not immediately apparent, science proves that our brains change as we learn. Without training the brain, our performance will tend to slow down, become less responsive and more susceptible to disease over time. Reading books is a great way to gain knowledge and stimulate creativity. Just like meditation, reading a book can have a calming effect and can improve focus. Not all books have the same effect, for example non-fiction books are great for broadening your horizons by motivating you and helping to develop new ideas. It has been proven that people who continue to learn will have faster responses, better social skills, help fight dementia, improve memory skills, make it easier to process new information and make you more productive

CREATE SOCIAL CONNECTIONS WITH POSITIVE PEOPLE.

Maybe most people prefer to enjoy alone time, but did you know that if you want to add more positive experiences to your life, then you need to have some strong social ties and community support. Social relationships not only give you pleasure, but also affect your long-term health. It is as important as nutrition, sleep and exercise. You should not be able to do bad habits in the name of socializing, because this will have a very bad impact on your future. The people you love and care about should be at the top of the list because they are the ones you can rely on when stress hits or life gets tougher to go through. It doesn't matter what you're working on or focused on in life, as long as you can set those priorities. The time set aside for the people you love should be cherished. In the end, if your time on earth is over, how will you be remembered?

How to Build a Social Circle Full of Positive People

Attracting quality people starts with taking responsibility for your actions and how they affect those around you.

Whether looking to build stronger relationships with the good people you already know or add more high-value friends into your life, attracting quality people starts with taking responsibility for your actions and how they affect those around you and who you attract. Understanding the qualities to cultivate within yourself will lead the right people to naturally gravitate toward you.

It's a two-way street.

What you are, you attract. If we expect quality people to want to spend time with us, we'll need to exhibit quality behaviors in return. That means evaluating the way we treat the people in our lives. No one is perfect, but we should focus on cultivating quality behaviors if we expect anyone to treat us in the same way.

Build better interpersonal skills.

Every relationship is only as good as the people in it so you'll want to work on qualities that help build stronger connections with others. That means developing interpersonal skills like active listening, paying attention, respect, honesty, and acceptance.

Lend a helping hand.

The Dalai Lama once said, "generosity is the most natural outward expression of an inner attitude of compassion and loving-kindness." Giving to others, whether money, time, or expertise, is a great way of showing others that we care. While you should give without the expectation of something in return, giving will also inspire kindness in others and attract generous people into our lives.

Develop a positive attitude.

Do you find the glass half-full or half-empty? Sure, it's an old cliche, but developing a positive outlook has many proven benefits that, not only make it easier to get through life but also attract quality people. Our attitude affects those around us. Quality people will naturally avoid negativity. So if you want to attract positive people, make sure you also have a positive perspective.

Smile!

"When you're smiling, the whole world smiles with you." Aside from having tons of health benefits like relieving stress, lowering blood pressure, and building a strong immune system, smiling also attracts more people and makes you more likable. Simply smiling brings the opportunity of meeting someone new.

Put yourself out there.

While it may not always seem easy to open up, you can't meet new, quality people without putting yourself out there. That might mean going out of your comfort zone. Look for events where you could easily meet people who share common interests. If you like to exercise, attend a workout class. If you like art, check out the new exhibition in town. By putting yourself out there, you'll have the chance to connect with new people.

Quality people lift each other up.

Surround yourself with people who lift you up, support you in your goals, and give you encouragement. Let's say you have a new business idea or weight loss goal. You'll want the people around you to say things like "That sounds amazing!" or "How can I help?" At the same time, you'll want to do the same for those around you as they focus on their new endeavors.

Learning when to let go.

Of course, sometimes even when we develop good behaviors within ourselves, we can let the good in with the bad. It's important to keep in mind that not everyone is worth our time. Giving time and energy to the wrong people can bring us down. In that case, we should learn when to let go of toxic relationships and walk away.

PRACTICE MINIMALISM.

Don't worry, no need to pack up your things and live your life as it is. The point here is that you may have a lot of things and that can have a negative impact on your life. We usually have a habitual cycle of collecting, displaying, moving, cleaning and finally storing the item in the warehouse. When you get rid of things that are at least rarely used or needed, then you can get a simple, neat environment and life. Life is short and it can get busy with sensory overload. Imagine all the distractions of stuff, relationships, work, stress, and bills all at once. Minimalism declares your life to be having more space for the things that are important to make you happy. When you spend less on buying and replacing items, you can save more in return. A minimalist lifestyle can also make your home easier to clean, time is easier to manage and life is easier to live in the future.

How to Practice Minimalism

Minimalism is the practice of removing everything unnecessary and focusing only on the things that really add value. It can be applied to a lot of areas — minimalist art and design are well established and have long histories. However, these days incorporating minimalism into your lifestyle is rapidly becoming the next big thing.

Doubtless you would have heard of Marie Kondo and her Netflix show, which is based on her popular book "The Life-Changing Magic of Tidying Up." Other key figures in the minimalist lifestyle movement are Joshua Fields Millburn and Ryan Nicodemus, who call themselves minimalists and have written books, made films and hosted podcasts on how to live a minimalist lifestyle. They also have a popular blog that shares tips and tricks on how to remove the clutter from your life.

At first glance, the concept of minimalism seems simple. Just get rid of everything you don't need. But often, we are too busy and stressed to take the time to figure out what we truly need in our lives and what we keep around as distractions. There is also a misconception that minimalism means just getting rid of all your furniture, painting your walls white, and putting in a wooden table and chair. There is a growing industry dedicated to selling you things that will help you maintain a minimalist lifestyle — but doesn't buying more things go against the basic concept of minimalism?

At its core, minimalism is about focusing your life only on the things that add value. Whether it's your home, work, school, or social life, you can use the principles of minimalism to make your daily life a more fulfilling one. Keep in mind that minimalism is not the magic solution to all of your life's problems. It is just a foundation on which you can build other good habits and practices to improve the quality of your life.

Here's how you can incorporate minimalism into your everyday routine. It's not difficult, and the more you do it the easier it will be to extend the approach to other aspects of your life as well.

Home. No, you don't need to throw out everything you own and live like a monk. But let's be honest, there are probably an awful lot of things in your house that you haven't looked at or touched in years. These are the things you need to be throwing out. As Marie Kondo's now-viral catchphrase goes, if it doesn't "spark joy", throw it out. Just because it's old, doesn't mean it's unnecessary. If an old letter or diary sparks joy, then keep it. But if a new sweatshirt or pair of shoes doesn't, then don't be afraid to get rid of it. Don't wait around for acts of nature to prompt you into starting the decluttering process — there's no time like the present!

Relationships. Getting rid of the toxic people in your life can go a long way to decluttering your social life and giving you peace of mind. We've all got an acquaintance or two that we just hate hanging out with because they just leave us feeling bad when the day ends. Don't be afraid to jettison these people from your lives. Some relationships are just not meant to be. Channel the energy you use to maintain these superficial ties into the relationships that you really care about. In relationships, as with most other things, it's about quality rather than quantity. Better to have a handful of really good, trustworthy friends than a whole collection of "friends" that don't add anything to your life.

Time. Time is finite, and many of us often find that we don't have enough of it to focus on the things we want to do. Take a look at your daily schedule and objectively evaluate how many of the items on there are really related to your interests and wishes. Don't be afraid to skip an office function or a school reunion every now and again if it really doesn't interest you.

Work. Try not to let your work bleed into the rest of your day. We spend most of our time in the office anyway, so make sure that when you're off-work, you're really off-work. Try not to check your work email or reply to work related messages outside office hours. This will help you make sure that you're maximizing your free time to enrich your own life as much as possible.

Minimalism is not an aesthetic. There's no fixed way to do it, no right or wrong answer, no set of rules that you have to follow. Read up about what it's really about and how people have used it throughout history. Then, look at your own life and see how best you can apply it in a way that suits your specific context. Most importantly, don't be afraid to start small — every little counts.